Essential Tips for the Inc
Secondary Classroom

This go-to resource provides practitioners with quick, easy and cost-effective ways of improving inclusive practices in educational settings.

Addressing the needs of children with various disabilities, from ADHD, dyslexia and low literacy skills, to physical disabilities, mental health and social needs, the book offers practitioners tips and ideas for ensuring that each and every student is integrated and supported to maximum effect. Clearly presented, concisely written and easily implemented, tips relate to critical elements of the school setting, including:

- the school environment and classroom organisation
- teaching equipment and resources
- lesson structures and timings
- early recognition and collaboration with families
- student–practitioner interaction and peer relationships.

Tips can be photocopied for display on staffroom noticeboards and circulated to colleagues. Engaging and accessible, this book will be an essential resource for practitioners, SENCOs and Inclusion Managers working in primary and secondary settings.

Pippa Whittaker is currently Head of Inclusion at a diverse inner-city secondary school in Bristol, UK.

Rachael Hayes is an Educational Psychologist, who is currently working for a Local Authority in the South West of England, UK.

nasen is a professional membership association that supports all those who work with or care for children and young people with special and additional educational needs. Members include teachers, teaching assistants, support workers, other educationalists, students and parents.

nasen supports its members through policy documents, journals, its magazine *Special*, publications, professional development courses, regional networks and newsletters. Its website contains more current information such as responses to government consultations. **nasen's** published documents are held in very high regard both in the UK and internationally.

For a full list of titles see: www.routledge.com/nasen-spotlight/book-series/ FULNASEN

Other titles published in association with the National Association for Special Educational Needs (nasen):

Essential Tips for the Inclusive Secondary Classroom
Pippa Whittaker and Rachael Hayes
2018/pb 978-1-138-06501-7

Time to Talk: Implementing outstanding practice in speech, language and communication, 2ed
Jean Gross
2018/pb 978-1-138-28054-0

The Post-16 SENCO Handbook: An essential guide to policy and practice
Elizabeth Ramshaw
2017/pb 978-1-138-65465-5

Supporting Children with Behaviour Issues in the Classroom, 2ed
Sarah Carr, Susan Coulter, Elizabeth Morling and Hannah Smith
2017/pb 978-1-138-67385-4

Supporting Children with Cerebral Palsy, 2ed
Rob Grayson, Jillian Wing, Hannah Tusiine, Graeme Oxtoby and Elizabeth Morling
2017/pb 978-1-138-18742-9

More Trouble with Maths: A teacher's complete guide to identifying and diagnosing mathematical difficulties, 2ed
Steve Chinn
2016/pb 978-1-138-18750-4

Supporting Children with Dyslexia, 2ed
Hilary Bohl and Sue Hoult
2016/pb 978-1-138-18561-6

Essential Tips for the Inclusive Secondary Classroom

A Road Map to Quality-first Teaching

Pippa Whittaker and
Rachael Hayes

Routledge
Taylor & Francis Group

LONDON AND NEW YORK

First published 2018
by Routledge
2 Park Square, Milton Park, Abingdon, Oxon OX14 4RN

and by Routledge
711 Third Avenue, New York, NY 10017

Routledge is an imprint of the Taylor & Francis Group, an informa business

British Library Cataloguing-in-Publication Data
A catalogue record for this book is available from the British Library

Library of Congress Cataloging-in-Publication Data
A catalog record for this book has been requested

ISBN: 978-1-138-06499-7 (hbk)
ISBN: 978-1-138-06501-7 (pbk)
ISBN: 978-1-315-16007-8 (ebk)

Typeset in Bembo
by Florence Production Ltd, Stoodleigh, Devon, UK

This book is dedicated to the very many exceptional children and young people in our schools, and to the fantastic staff who are working so hard to support them.

Key to tips

Introduction

Often in schools we talk at length about concepts such as inclusion, differentiation and Quality First Teaching, without having enough practical strategies to make these concepts a reality in the classroom. This little book provides an easy way to develop Quality First Teaching in your own classroom, or across the whole school.

For teachers: You can 'dip in' to the book at any point to find a quick and easy tip to help you fine-tune your practice and support students' learning. If you are looking for strategies on a specific topic (such as ADHD or Dyslexia) then use the finger tabs to find tips that are specific to that topic.

For school leaders: This book contains 190 tips, one for every day of the school year, for you to share with your staff as a quick and easy way of developing Quality First Teaching. The pages can be scanned and e-mailed to all staff, or copied and displayed on a staff noticeboard, or even shared verbally at your staff briefing.

When you are planning your seating plans, consider learners with ADHD and ASC first. What are the 'prime' positions in your classroom, where they can be seated away from distractions such as 'busy' displays, windows with a view and lively peers? It will be fruitful to invest some time at the start of term planning seating around their attentional and sensory needs in order to minimise difficulties later on.

Learners with ADHD and ASC tend to settle better in a predictable and uncluttered environment, so why not use the start of a new term as an opportunity to have a quick tidy and de-clutter of your classroom? Ideally, the wall where the whiteboard hangs will be as empty and uncluttered as possible to support focus and concentration, and displays of work and 'working walls' can be kept for the other three walls in the room.

Learners with Dyspraxia are more likely to get lost, even in buildings that they are used to. Be patient if this happens and they are late, and, if possible, take time to prepare them for any errands or journeys that are out of their routine. Take a moment to share with them a mental map of where they need to go, or if possible make sure they have a simple map so that they can self-check where they need to go.

DATE SHARED

When you are teaching new ideas and vocabulary, make sure you revisit these every lesson until they are absolutely secure. Too often, we teach an idea or piece of information and then move on, never cementing it to the point at which it is automatic nor properly integrated into learners' prior knowledge. Creating a 'working wall' of words learned this lesson, this week, this term and this year, and revisiting these until they are absolutely secure, is a really useful way of ensuring that all words are revisited and kept current rather than being forgotten as soon as a learner leaves your classroom!

Research shows that a good mental health and wellbeing is crucial if we are to flourish and be resilient to life's setbacks. Yet nationally, 1 in 10 children aged 5–16 are found to have a diagnosable mental health disorder – that is an average of three learners in every class. If you have concerns about a learner's mental health or wellbeing, it is vital that you raise this with the appropriate pastoral staff at the earliest opportunity so that the right support can be put in place.

If you feel that a learner is at risk of harm due to their state of mental health, or if you become aware that harm has already happened, then you should raise this as an urgent safeguarding concern as soon as is possible.

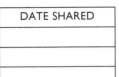

DATE SHARED

Learners with Dyscalculia will greatly benefit from the use of concrete aids or pictorial representations of numbers in all subjects where they are using mathematical operations or counting skills. For example, this could include counters, blocks and so on. You will need to model how they can use these materials or pictures to carry out the task – don't just assume that it is obvious to them what they need to do – talk them through what the materials or pictures represent and how they can manipulate these to help them with the operation or task.

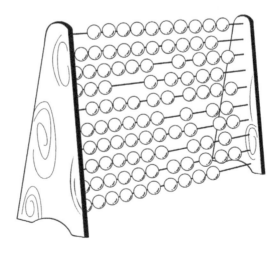

If you have additional adults supporting in your lessons, please try to find a moment to share learning objectives and activities with them. You could do this by: e-mailing or giving them unit plans at the start of the unit; meeting with them once a short term for ten minutes or so to talk through the plans for the term; sharing your session plan with them when they come into the classroom; taking a moment to talk to them during the lesson so that they know what they key learning points are. The more communication can take place, the more effective the in-class support and therefore the quality of learning is likely to be.

If you are teaching a class with a number of children who have SEMH, at times it can feel as though maintaining peace and calm is an uphill climb! Give yourself an advantage by setting expectations for positive social behaviours from the outset. Even better, work with your class to create a class charter of expectations of themselves and each other, have everyone sign it, and display it in the room. It is not likely to solve all the difficulties, but does give you a shared framework to refer back to when you give specific positive praise, or when dealing with social issues or conflicts.

A 'working wall' can be a great way of supporting lots of learners, but particularly those who have EAL or literacy difficulties such as Dyslexia. It can also support the conceptual understanding of learners with MLD. Pictures, key words, work samples, and diagrams can all help to underpin key ideas and language. Examples of notes and work in progress can also emphasise to learners that development of ideas is ongoing, and quality and improvement is more important than presentation! A web search for 'working wall' will give you lots of ideas for a 'working wall' in your classroom.

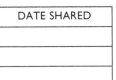

DATE SHARED

Learners with Dyspraxia, Dyslexia, Visual Impairment and more general fine motor difficulties often find it extremely difficult to 'keep within the lines' on narrow-lined paper. Where possible, give them the option of wide-lined paper – this can have a very positive impact on the handwriting and presentation of work, and therefore in their pride in their work and engagement with learning.

It is perfectly normal for newly-arrived learners with EAL to go through a 'silent period', which may last anything between a few days and several months. Do not pressure them into speaking before they feel ready; instead, aim to encourage the use of low-key non-verbal cues such as nodding, thumbs up or showing a green / amber / red card to let you know if they've understood. Pairing them with a peer with the same first language can also help during these early weeks and months.

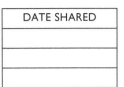

DATE SHARED

If a student with SEMH should try to leave your classroom, then never stand in their way by blocking the doorway. This is likely to result in an escalation of their emotional state and yours, and could result in physical harm to both of you. Instead, allow them to leave and use the usual school systems to ensure that they are picked up and allowed time to calm down. Then make plans or reparations to mend the situation once they are in a fit state of mind to do so.

© 2018 *Essential Tips for the Inclusive Secondary Classroom*, Whittaker, Hayes, Routledge

It can be useful to familiarise yourself with the current terminology of hearing impairment so that you can confidently and sensitively discuss learners' needs with them, their parents and other staff with confidence and sensitivity. The phrase 'people with hearing loss' is used to describe people with a whole range of hearing impairments, as is the phrase 'people who are deaf'. Both these phrases include those who are profoundly deaf. 'Hard of hearing' is usually used to refer to people who have mild to severe hearing loss. People's level of deafness is defined using the terms mild, moderate, severe or profound. Many people with hearing loss will need different types of 'communication support' and you will need to make sure you are aware of any communication support that your learners need.

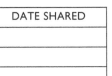

Quality displays have the potential to really underpin learning for all learners, especially those with additional needs! The best displays are those that are kept tidy and current, and that include quality work samples across the ability range, engaging pictures, key words, success criteria and tactile / multi-sensory objects that underpin key ideas.

A good strategy to support learners with learning, attentional or memory difficulties to work more independently is to prepare a short video clip of the target skills, which they can then rewatch during the lesson without needing to ask you. For example, in a Science lesson this might include a short clip saved onto an iPad or laptop of heating a test tube over a Bunsen burner. These clips can even be prepared by your learners as a 'stretch and challenge' activity and saved in a bank of 'self-help' clips for use in future lessons.

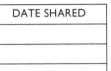

Learners with physical disabilities have a legal right to be included in all areas of the curriculum, including practical subjects such as PE, Drama, Science and DT. We should never assume that learners with physical disabilities and impairments are not able to take part, but instead we need to be prepared to spend time planning what they can do, including adjusted activities, the use of supportive aids and equipment, additional adult support or a peer buddy, where necessary. The Code of Practice for SEND is explicit that teachers need to take responsibility for this, but of course this can be in liaison with the learners themselves and with advice from the SENCO.

Some learners have sensory sensitivities that result in them being either over- or under- sensitive to specific senses. For example, learners with an over-sensitivity to touch may find certain textures or types of material or fabric unbearable – this can include scratchy labels in school jumpers, for example, or the feeling of a tie that is tight around their neck. However, learners with an under-sensitivity may deliberately seek the stimulation of touch; they might enjoy the feeling of being underneath heavy objects, or of self-harming behaviours or of chewing objects. Be aware of any learners who have these sensitivities by liaising with the SENCO, remembering what they find difficult and being prepared to be flexible in your expectations.

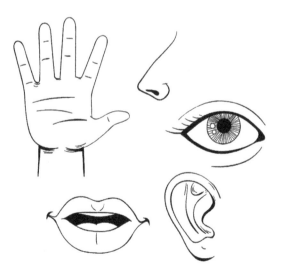

Gesture and mime is an extremely powerful way of communicating to learners with EAL and many with SEND; it underpins the meaning of your spoken communication and engages listeners in a way that talk on its own is not able to do. Start by using gesticulation and mime for common classroom activities such as writing, opening your book, thinking, looking and listening. Note the response of your learners with additional needs – are they more attentive and better able to access what you are telling them? If so, continue with this and think about how you can further broaden these cues in your next lesson.

© 2018 *Essential Tips for the Inclusive Secondary Classroom*, Whittaker, Hayes, Routledge

Language can be very powerful in ensuring a calm and boundaried classroom environment. One simple example of this is following instructions with the word 'thanks' rather than 'please', which alters the tone from that of a request or plea, to an instruction where it is assumed that they will comply with what is being asked. Another example is responding to a learner who is trying to enter into a confrontation or argument with a calm response along the lines of 'Right, well I will want to discuss that with you in a moment'. This is a confident response that avoids entering into a debate in front of an audience, defuses the confrontation, shows that you are confidently in charge and not rattled by the challenge and shows the class that you will be dealing with it in time.

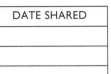

DATE SHARED

While all of your learners will be aged eleven and above, there are likely to be a number of learners in your classes who have a reading age below this, in some cases significantly so. Aim to find out the reading ages of your groups and support your learners to access texts in your lessons by: increasing text size and spacing, changing font from Times New Roman to Arial or Comic Sans, adding picture clues, reading to them, simplifying language, shortening sentences, reducing the amount of text and using pastel-coloured backgrounds to reduce visual glare.

Writing frames can provide a very useful 'scaffold' for learners with literacy, language and Learning Difficulties, or who have English as an Additional Language. There are lots of adaptable writing frames online and you can easily search for this by genre – e.g. 'writing frame for scientific report', 'writing frame for factual recount' and so on. While it is not a good idea to rely on these as the only route into extended writing – shared generating of ideas and planning is essential – writing frames can be very helpful for those who struggle to get started on a piece of work and therefore are a useful back up in the classroom.

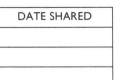

DATE SHARED

Learners with Visual Impairments need to be seated appropriately if they are to be able to access lessons. Please take a moment to check that visually impaired learners you teach can see you and the board – don't presume that they will tell you if they can't see! If you are not sure about the best position for any individuals, then liaise with the Learning Support Team.

Learners who have family members with disabilities and additional needs may find themselves taking on extra caring responsibilities. This can have a huge impact on their life as they often have to support with practical tasks, such as cooking, cleaning, laundry and caring for siblings, as well as practical mobility support. This can make it very difficult for them to find time to complete homework. Please be sensitive to this fact and, where possible, talk to learners individually to see what support or adjustments might help.

DATE SHARED

What makes the difference for young people who've been through trauma is the quality of trusting relationships that they are able to form with adults in school. Take time this week to invest in relationships with your most challenged young people – actively make eye contact, ask how they are, chat with them for a bit. If you can repeat these actions over a period of days, weeks and months, you are very likely to see an improvement in the quality of your connection and in their engagement in your lessons.

During listening tasks or film clips, learners with attentional difficulties such as ADHD will need a clear structure to help them focus. This could be: specific information or facts to listen out for and note down, a page to highlight key words they hear (like bingo), or a simple grid to fill in with key ideas like 'who, what, why and where'.

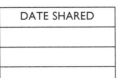

DATE SHARED

Many learners with ASC can be sensitive to noises, textures, smells and sights that we might not even notice – such as the smell of other children, dirt or grit on the desk, humming of the lights, the brightness of certain classrooms, smells from cookery rooms and 'unusual' textures such as paints, playdough, labels in uniform, socks and so on. It is worth being aware of these additional stressors and the fact that they can feel quite all-consuming for some learners with ASC.

It is worth asking them what they notice about your room in terms of distractions – the responses can be surprising. If you can, take five minutes at the end of the day to reflect on the 'sensory clutter' in your classroom and think about whether you can reduce any of it in any way ready for tomorrow.

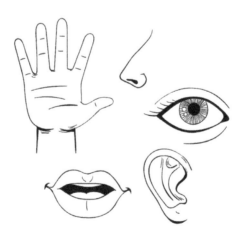

Don't wait until things are 'going wrong' with a learner who has SEN before you ask for advice! Your school's TAs and Learning Support Team have a wealth of experience about what works for the learners they support as they see learners across the range of subjects and are able to observe how they respond to a wide range of strategies and approaches. Do approach them for suggestions as they will often be very happy to discuss ideas and come up with some strategies that you can try out.

Many learners can benefit from written and pictorial instructions, rather than instructions, which are only given verbally. This doesn't require any pre-preparation – you can explain a task to the class and then write the key points together in summary using simple language on the whiteboard. Writing the key points together like this will both reinforce information to learners as well as checking their understanding. This strategy is particularly useful for learners with memory difficulties, EAL, ASC, Dyslexia, Dyscalculia and ADHD.

© 2018 *Essential Tips for the Inclusive Secondary Classroom*, Whittaker, Hayes, Routledge

About 20% of Dyslexic learners find it much easier to read from pastel-coloured paper, or using coloured overlays, both of which reduce visual glare compared to white paper. If you have any Dyslexic learners in your lessons, take a moment to find out what colours they find easiest and aim to consistently provide them in your lessons as an inclusive strategy.

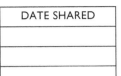

DATE SHARED

Learners with motor and literacy difficulties such as Dyslexia and Dyspraxia often struggle to write clearly and fluidly using cheap, poor quality pens. This kind of pen can require a lot of physical effort to produce a thin and scratchy letter shape, which doesn't invoke any feeling of pride in a learner's handwriting and nor does it promote good presentation.

If possible, make time and space for learners to try different types of pen (e.g. fountain pen, fineliner, ink pen) and, if they have a clear preference, you can then raise this as a recommendation with parents at parents' evening or see what you can make available from school stock.

Many learners, including those with MLD and SEMH needs, engage really well with opportunities to evidence their learning in ways other than writing. For example, this could include taking photographs of themselves demonstrating key ideas, which they then print and caption; model making using plasticine or Lego; drawing diagrams or mind maps of ideas and concepts; spoken presentations, which can be taped or filmed. These strategies can be used as an alternative for key learners or as a way to provide variety and increase engagement for the whole class. This evidence can then be kept in books or referred on to in your marking, as a way of capturing knowledge and understanding and with the same quality feedback as you would give to written work, with a focus on moving learning forward.

Learners who have experienced early trauma or relationship difficulties may often experience behaviourist approaches, such as being given consequences, as an indication of how they can 'get on your nerves' and push your emotional buttons. This may then mean that they are more likely to repeat the poor behaviours as they are then rewarded by your attention and reaction, even if it is negative. Therefore, as well as using the school behaviour systems, try also to invest in using supportive strategies and building a relationship with them, as it is this that is likely to effect more lasting impact. Focus on sharing interests with them, find ways to reward them with positive attention, make eye contact and ask how they are, tune in to how they might be feeling.

When you are talking to a learner with a hearing loss or impairment, always turn to face them straight on so that they can lipread if they need to. Don't assume that a hearing aid means they have perfect hearing and therefore won't need face-to-face contact. Speak clearly, slowly and naturally, as exaggerating sounds can make lipreading more difficult.

The most common mental health difficulties you are likely to encounter in your classroom are depression and anxiety, which affects nearly 8% of the population at any one time. Learners with these conditions will need additional support and understanding if their condition is to stabilise and improve. Furthermore, many formally diagnosed mental health difficulties are classed as disabilities, and therefore schools are required by law to make 'reasonable adjustments' for these conditions under the Equality Act. Examples of reasonable adjustments might include: being allowed to do 'speaking and listening' assessments with the teacher or a small group, rather than in front of the class; being allowed access to a smaller room for exams, if the exam hall situation provokes anxiety; being treated with sensitivity rather than with a punitive approach, if homework is a particular source of anxiety.

For learners with memory difficulties, you can reduce the demands on their auditory systems by providing visual cues as you teach. This can include pointing to relevant pages and prompts around the room, using picture prompts drawn on the board or on a PowerPoint, and giving models of what you want them to achieve, on paper, to refer to as they work.

In your classroom, there will be learners with a range of reading abilities: those who can read the words off the page (decode) and understand what they mean (comprehend); those who can decode but have poor comprehension, those who can comprehend but have poor decoding skills and those who struggle with both decoding and comprehension. If you have learners who are struggling with reading text in your lessons, it is worth considering their difficulties in more detail so you can tailor strategies to support them. For example, learners with poor comprehension will need pre-teaching of key words / ideas, thought storming of the text's key points and pictures to underpin meaning. Learners with poor decoding but good comprehension need paired reading or teacher reading and highlighting key words in advance. Learners in need of support with both decoding and comprehension will benefit from all these strategies, as well as targeted questioning to check understanding.

When you are talking to your class, be mindful of the language you use when referring to people with learning difficulties and disabilities. Terms such as 'handicapped', 'slow', 'needy' and 'weak' are rightly considered derogatory of people with additional needs. Be prepared to respectfully challenge terms such as these when students or staff use them!

Some learners have sensory sensitivities that make it virtually impossible for them to concentrate if there are distracting noises, smells or visuals in the classroom. Often these stimuli are things that others might not even notice, such as a pen tapping or the humming of a projector. While you may not be able to eradicate all these stimuli, there is a lot you can do to help learners who have sensory sensitivities. For example, advance preparation can be helpful: if you know that there is going to be a new noise, such as a musical recital in the hall next door or hedge trimming outside, you can give advance warning to those who are likely to find this distracting or overloading. If extended concentration is needed, you might allow them to work away from the stimulus, maybe at an individual workstation or even in the departmental office, if appropriate.

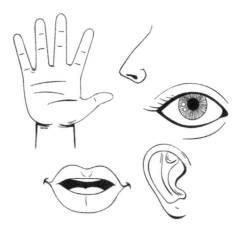

As teachers, we often use thought storms, spider diagrams and mind maps to construct simple frameworks of information. However, there is great potential to use concept maps to construct frameworks of even the most complex information, and to use them to show interconnection between topics. Research suggests that high-quality concept mapping is one of the most effective ways there is to learn. Take time to teach your learners the skill of concept mapping – the work of educationalist Tony Buzan is a great starting point.

DATE SHARED

For learners whose behaviour can be challenging, relationship between schools, student and families can become increasingly strained when all contact home is about poor behaviour.

Try to find a couple of moments each week to make a quick phone call home for learners who are really making an effort with their behaviour in your subject – this can make all the difference to securing positive parental support!

Sometimes learners can be resistant to reading, but there is a lot we, as teachers and support staff, can do to encourage a love of reading. Whenever possible we should aim to include reading for enjoyment in our lessons and tutor times. Make reading fun and non-threatening by reading to learners and asking for volunteers to read a section each aloud, rather than insisting that everyone reads a section, which is hugely stressful for many poor readers. Finally, we can tell our learners with enthusiasm about the books we are enjoying at home and celebrate learners' reading efforts and successes with equal enthusiasm.

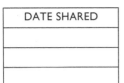

DATE SHARED

Learners with Visual Impairments will benefit from well laid out and clearly printed resources. Ideally text will be uncluttered and clear fonts such as Comic Sans or Arial will be used; you could also consider double line spacing. Some learners will need resources to be enlarged – if you are unsure whether this is the case for a student you are working with, then liaise with the SENCO as appropriate.

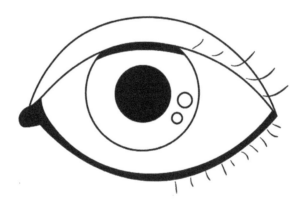

If you want a learner to focus on a particular activity for a limited period of time (such as writing for ten minutes), reduce the levels of noise and visual distraction in the classroom to help them concentrate. This can be done by using headphones, for example, to block out sounds, seating them away from distraction in the room and by having the whole class working in silence. These strategies are likely to make a real impact for learners with attentional difficulties such as ADHD.

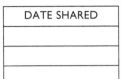

DATE SHARED

Learners with ASC, EAL and MLD can really benefit from visual timetables showing the routine for the lesson, the day or the whole week. Visual timetables can be very simple and include picture icons and words to show key places, routines and actions. If learners have a clear idea what to do and where to go at a given time, they are less likely to get stressed or to be late to lessons. Therefore, visual timetables can be powerful tools to reduce levels of dependence and anxiety and make daily life much easier and more enjoyable for everyone involved!

When planning for personalised learning, make sure that each session includes opportunities for more challenge (higher-order thinking for the most-able learners) and less challenge (lower-order thinking for the less-able learners), rather than just more or less of the same kind of work. Bloom's Taxonomy is an invaluable tool in planning activities that cover the whole range of challenge!

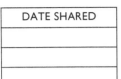

DATE SHARED

Learners with Dyscalculia need processes to be broken down into 'small chunks' so that they can succeed. Teach and remind them as they are working to encourage a graduated approach to solving problems, which includes showing all working out. Adjust the number of problems they are expected to solve in a given time, as this will give them more time to solve each problem using the graduated approach you have taught them and will reduce anxiety and stress.

234 + 135

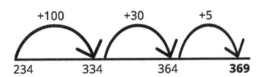

Or

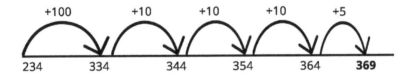

Key word lists with pictures for each word are a valuable resource for supporting writing in all subject areas. They are so useful for learners with many needs, including those with literacy difficulties such as Dyslexia, those with EAL, and those with Learning Difficulties. The most sustainable way to develop these is to make them for each topic at the stage of departmental planning and print and laminate them so that they can be re-used.

There is much that you can do to help learners with Dyspraxia to produce their clearest writing. Make sure that their seating position is suitable for their hand dominance, so, for example, do not seat a left-handed student next to a right-handed one as this can be very intrusive for both. Writing slopes can also make a real difference as there is less physical strain than when writing on a flat surface, such as a desk. If a writing slope is not available, or if a student is embarrassed to be seen using one, consider an A4 ring binder as an alternative. This is an adjustment that you could easily offer to all of your class – it is very likely that there will also be other learners for whom it improves the quality and ease of their writing.

To ensure that newly-arrived learners with EAL feel welcomed, consider learning some simple words and phrases in the learners' first language, using these and encouraging other learners to use them in the classroom. Your efforts – however small – are likely to be greatly appreciated and will really help you to build a relationship with your newly-arrived EAL learners.

DATE SHARED	

Some learners struggle to show how they are feeling and can appear very shy and quiet in the classroom. This can be interpreted either as disengagement, or as the absence of any difficulty, even though they may be struggling but not feel able to express this. Have a think about learners in your classes who fit this profile – what can you do to open a dialogue with them about how things are going? Could you let them know what behaviour they can show if they want your help e.g. displaying a card on their desk, putting their head on the table or another non-verbal cue? This will improve your responsiveness to their needs and support their learning progress.

© 2018 *Essential Tips for the Inclusive Secondary Classroom*, Whittaker, Hayes, Routledge

If you have learners with a hearing impairment, it is vital that you ensure background noise is kept to a minimum. Insist on silence during teacher talk or class discussion time, otherwise it can be very difficult for learners with hearing loss to differentiate speech sound against background noise. Similarly, be mindful of 'other' background noise that you can reduce, such as blinds on an open window banging against the wall or echoes down a corridor when the door is ajar.

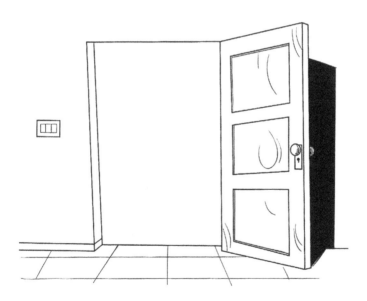

There is a strong and proven link between bullying in schools and mental health difficulties. Be vigilant to bullying in your classroom – not only verbal or physical abuse but also more subtle abuse such as learners being excluded from groups and activities, ignored or treated with disdain and others being encouraged to do the same. All forms of bullying need to be treated as serious so that learners know they are not accepted in school. It can be very powerful to make learners aware that you have observed what is happening and that it is not acceptable and that you will be passing it on to relevant senior leaders. This can contribute to school feeling like a safer place for all learners, particularly those who are socially vulnerable.

Where learners are supported by additional adults such as TAs, always try to find a moment for direct communication in the lesson between the teacher and the student. Research shows that content is lost when all communication is routed via the additional adult and it also makes it more difficult for the subject teacher to accurately gauge progress and understanding. Learners who have a greater amount of direct communication and challenge from the teacher make much better progress than those for whom most instructions and content always arrive second-hand via their supporting adult.

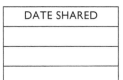

Aim to spend five minutes this week carrying out a 'walk through' of your classroom to make sure it is as accessible as possible for learners with physical disabilities. For example, do these learners have access to the 'best' seats in the room – those with a clear, head-on view of the board or are they limited to the poorer seats at edge of a room with a sideways view of the board? Or maybe their peers are able to sit in friendship groups, but those seats and tables are not accessible for learners with physical disabilities so they are inadvertently excluded? If so, is there any way you can adjust the furniture and layout so that learners with physical disabilities have access to the very best learning opportunities in your lessons?

DATE SHARED

Learners with sensory processing and attentional difficulties can be distracted by having too much information displayed on the walls around the board. If possible, avoid 'busy' displays at the front of your room and only have key information on boards. If you want to be able to share examples of good quality work, then you can keep these in a folder. You can have separate folders for topics and year groups or scan the work and share it electronically.

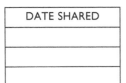

Learners who are Young Carers are often embarrassed or ashamed of the additional responsibilities that they may have at home and they may not want peers or teachers to be aware. Be sensitive to this and make sure that any conversations about e.g. attendance at parents' evenings or missed homework, happens out of the ear shot of other learners so that their dignity and privacy is maintained.

Always take time to pre-teach key vocabulary before you use it in context. This can be either at the start of a module of work or at the beginning of a lesson. Pre-teaching of vocabulary is powerful because it means that learners with SEND and EAL needs will be 'primed' for the key words and will be familiar with their sounds and meanings before they have to deal with them embedded into a wider language context.

DATE SHARED

Unconditional Positive Regard is a way of communicating our support and acceptance of a person, regardless of what they say or do. It may include phrasing feedback and instructions in such a way as to assume the best of them and to reinforce that we have high hopes for them! Examples might be: 'I remember how well you did this two lessons ago when . . .' and 'You always come into this room brilliantly – thank you for that'. This can sometimes be difficult with our learners who display the most oppositional behaviours, but it can be one way to develop relationships and share our high expectations in a respectful and positive way.

For more information on the notion of Unconditional Positive Regard, you can research the works of American psychologist Carl Rogers.

When you are introducing a new text in any subject, help your learners to 'cue in' to its meaning by spending some time explicitly focusing on and analysing the heading or title, any subheadings, any pictures or illustration, and the layout of the text on the page (e.g. is it written in columns like a newspaper? Is it presented as a webpage? Is it presented as a list of instructions, with numbers at the side? And so on). This helps learners to become more active readers by developing their ability to use genre cues to 'predict' what a text is going to be about and what style it will be written in, which in turn will help them to become competent and convincing writers. Good and experienced readers do this automatically, but most learners will need you to teach them how to do this.

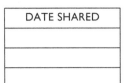

DATE SHARED

When word processing, most learners will automatically type in Times New Roman, font size 12 and on a white background. However, there are some simple adaptations that can make the process of writing much easier when using a word-processor. For example, adjusting the background to cream or a pale pastel colour can reduce visual glare, which can help many learners to read what they have written with less visual stress. A simpler font in a larger size, such as Arial or Comic Sans in font size 14 or 16, can also help as these are less visually 'fussy' than some other fonts. Teach your learners to choose between these options and explain why they may help and you may well see an improvement in both the quality and the quantity of their writing.

Eye tests are not routinely offered in secondary schools in the UK, meaning that there are likely to be learners in your classrooms at some point who have unidentified visual problems. Be aware of the signs of a visual problem and flag up any concerns with the learner's family, via the pastoral team if appropriate, so that they can be taken for an eye test. Signs to look out for include not only squinting and difficulty seeing the board, but also sensitivity to light and signs of eye pain, such as rubbing the eyes or complaining of painful eyes.

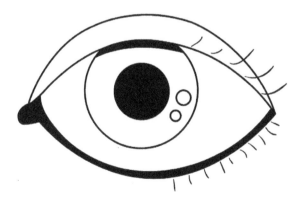

DATE SHARED

As much as possible, try to be mindful that some curriculum topics will be sensitive for some of your learners. This is particularly true for those who are looked-after, many of whom will have experienced trauma and abuse in the family setting, for those who are Young Carers or who have suffered bereavement and for learners who have been displaced from their home countries and are fleeing war or conflict. If you have concerns that a topic you are teaching may be difficult for a particular learner liaise with involved pastoral staff as well as having a pre-conversation with the learner to gain their views, to ascertain the best approach, may be appropriate.

If you want your class to work in silence for a set period of time, then there are a range of strategies that can help to make this happen, even with high levels of SEND. For example, you might think about: Using an on-screen timer to show the length of time and training the class by resetting it each time someone talks without good reason to. There are also online visual tools, which monitor the noise of the classroom using sound waves and visually demonstrate when the noise is becoming too loud – do a web search for 'ways to monitor classroom noise level' or 'noise meter for classrooms' for current examples. Finally, be realistic – for many groups, working in silence for an hour is simply unrealistic; instead, start with ten minutes and gradually increase this expectation over time.

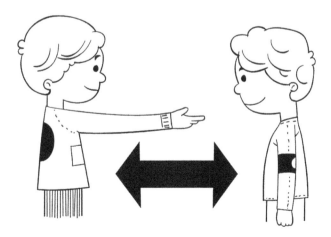

DATE SHARED

Learners with ASC, Sensory Needs and Dyspraxia may need your support to recognise where their body ends and to stay out of what others see as their own personal space. Organise your classroom to enable learners with these needs to sit with peers in such a way that their own working space is clearly demarcated and sufficient for them, so that they don't feel trapped or squashed. Speak with them about where feels most comfortable in the room and try to make sure that this is not changed without discussion, as this can cause anxiety.

Worksheets and lesson materials need to be as accessible as possible, as many learners with SEND and EAL will struggle to access resources with lots of text, fonts that are visually 'fussy' or too small, faded copies made from copies or on white paper, which can cause visual glare. Be prepared to try out different styles and size of font, colours of paper, varying amounts of text and pictures on the page, and talk to your class about how they find these.

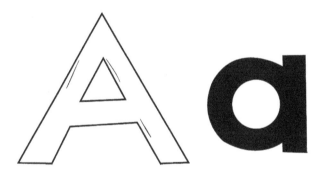

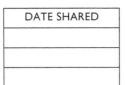

DATE SHARED

Learners with Dyscalculia and MLD are likely to benefit from explicit and repeated teaching of skills for estimation, comparison and summarising of number facts. Don't presume that they will have these skills in place already, as many will need overteaching of core concepts such as higher and lower, larger and smaller etc, in relation to number. Number games and class quizzes can help learners to master and retain these skills.

234 + 135

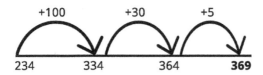

Or

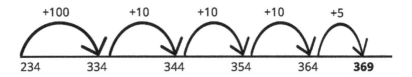

Learners with Dyslexia can easily become demotivated if every spelling mistake in their work is corrected. It is far more effective to correct only the first three high-frequency words that are spelled incorrectly, since these are common words that will be most useful for a student to expend time and energy learning. The high-frequency word lists can be found online.

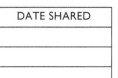

DATE SHARED

Wide-lined paper can make a huge difference to the quality and presentation of writing produced by learners with literacy difficulties and Dyspraxia. Most schools have wide-lined paper and books stored in department offices and learning support classrooms, so have a hunt around and see what you can find. Alternatively, there is lots of printable wide-lined paper online. Offer it to your learners and then assess whether there is any impact on the quality of their writing and the ease with which they can write.

DATE SHARED

Wherever possible, try to include elements of EAL learners' own cultures in your lesson planning as a way to ensure they know their experiences and cultures are valued in school – for example, you can include reference to foods from their home country in a DT lesson, athletes in a PE lesson or artists in an Art lesson.

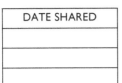

DATE SHARED

For learners with hearing impairments, the traditional 'rows of desks' classroom layout can be very challenging as it is not easy to see peers' faces when they contribute during the lesson. Consider a horseshoe layout for class discussions or questioning instead; this is much more inclusive of learners with hearing loss.

Mental health needs can only be formally diagnosed by medical professionals, and so it is important that teachers do not use terminology or diagnostic labels unless a formal diagnosis has been given. However, teachers are ideally placed to look out for signs and symptoms of mental health difficulties, such as a sudden change of mood or demeanour, or signs of self-harm or distress. If you have concerns about the emotional state of any student, always refer these through the usual pastoral and safeguarding channels in school, so that this can be noted and relevant support can be put in place.

DATE SHARED

Giving electronic positive points is not always tangible for the developmental level of learners with MLD as they are not visual or immediate enough, so they are unlikely to be motivating. However, there are some very simple ways to set up visual reward systems; for example, every time you see a positive behaviour in the class, you could put a coloured glass gem (available from household stores) in a plastic jar. When the jar is full, the class can choose a film for a 'mini cinema' event – you bring in a DVD and even some little packets of popcorn. Or you can give out 'raffle tickets' for great behaviours and choose a winning ticket at the end of the lesson – prizes could be as simple as leaving the classroom first for a week, not having to put chairs up or a choice of gel or highlighter pens – always a winner!

If any of your learners have a physical disability or visual impairment that makes it difficult for them to turn easily or see from an angle, you will need to make sure that you seat them where they can easily see the learning resources and displays in the classroom, otherwise they will be disadvantaged by having access to less information than their peers. Similarly, if you are using a 'working wall' with key words and visuals, make sure that learners with physical or visual impairments have the best seats for seeing this at near sight and face-on, again so that the barriers caused by their disabilities are removed as much as is possible.

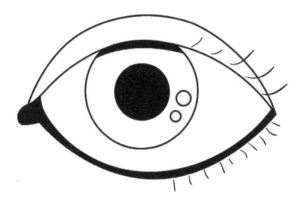

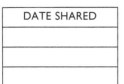

DATE SHARED

As good readers with good language comprehension, we naturally and subconsciously select the most important words – the content-carrying words – from any sentence we read or hear, and use these to develop our understanding of what the sentence is about. However, learners with language or learning difficulties, and those with EAL, will struggle to do this. We can help them by emphasising the key words for them. When reading or writing written text, we can underline, highlight or embolden the key words. When speaking or reading aloud, we can emphasise key words by saying these louder and more slowly, by repeating them and even draw extra attention to them by writing them on the board as we say them.

Quiet and anxious students can easily feel sidelined when they are working in groups with more confident and dominant peers. Think about how you will manage this to develop the skills of both groups. Consider giving out specific roles in the classroom to support with this – for example, a quieter student might benefit from a specific area of responsibility (such as classroom monitor), which can then encourage them to gradually interact with a wider range of peers, even if this is in a low-key way at first. Similarly, more dominant students might benefit from the role of scribe or chair, so that their success depends on listening to, facilitating and taking note of the views of those who are less vocal.

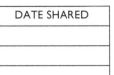
You can help your learners to become better readers and writers by explicitly teaching text types that are used in your subject. This teaching might include information about the expected layout, style of language, audience and purpose of each text type. For example, in Science, they are likely to need to be familiar with the conventions of a formal report; therefore, learners will need to be taught about the layout of a report, the style of language, the audience and so on. You can encourage learners to engage with these ideas by presenting them with a very poorly written report and encouraging them to analyse what is wrong with it – many of them will have a 'sense' that it is not right, but will benefit greatly developing a clear list of conventions that they can refer to as a reader and as a writer.

When you start your class on any kind of writing task, there is lots you can do to avoid that 'rabbit in the headlights' look that some learners will present you with, no matter how much detail you include in your explanation! Even a simple pair talk and class thought storm around 'what words and phrases will we need for our writing?' with the ideas displayed as they write, can go a long way to helping learners cue in to the type of language and genre that is needed for the task. Also, try to provide some sentence starters if possible or get the class to generate some options, as this can also help learners get over the initial 'hurdle' of starting to write.

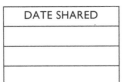

DATE SHARED

If you are showing film clips or using PowerPoint in the classroom, it is worth making sure that the lighting in the room is appropriate. The room should not be too dimly lit and it is important that there is no glare from the sun or from lights on the board. Learners with visual difficulties may not be able to see the materials you are presenting if there is visual glare or if the room generally is too dark.

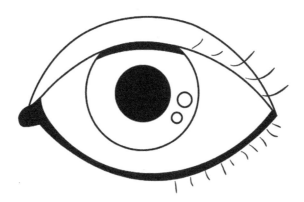

Learners who are Young Carers may, at times, need additional emotional support from an adult. Don't be afraid to check with them that they have someone to talk to in school and to refer them on to the pastoral team if they do not. Just knowing that adults are aware of them and can support them if needed – understanding their situation and being 'there for them' – can have a positive impact on the wellbeing of a young person during difficult periods.

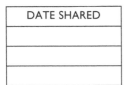

DATE SHARED

Planned movement breaks can make a huge difference for learners who struggle to sit still for longer periods, including those with ADHD. If you notice that a learner is struggling to maintain focus, considering asking them to run an errand, take a note to another staff member for you or to be in charge of putting something back or giving something out. This is likely to minimise disruption to the class, give them the break they need and allow you to praise them and keep the situation on a positive footing once the task has been completed.

Many learners with ASC, anxiety and SEMH may quickly feel anxious or demotivated if they are repeatedly unable to finish a task in the time given. This can particularly be the case with starters and plenary activities. Make sure that you plan tasks carefully for the time given, and that there is a differentiated version where necessary for learners who will need this. Be clear at the start how long learners have to complete a task and use a timer or stopwatch on the board so that timings are clear and transparent.

The right of all children to access inclusive mainstream education is enshrined in UN Human Rights legislation and the Equality Act 2010. In spite of this, many such young people and their families will have faced hostility and negativity in their dealings with staff in mainstream schools. While this may arise from a place of concern about meeting their needs, it is unlawful and, therefore, unacceptable. This is true of those with SEND, as well as EAL needs. Please make an extra effort to be welcoming and positive in your dealings with learners who have more complex needs and with their families. Always remember – this is their school and they have a right to be here. Make sure that all your interactions with them clearly communicate that you welcome them in your classroom and that they belong.

Many learners with SEND need support to set out Maths problems in a systematic way on the page; this can be particularly true for learners with MLD, Dyscalculia and Dyspraxia. You can scaffold this for them by giving them a worksheet with appropriate lines and boxes (like a flowchart or number frame), which provide a systemic framework for solving the problem – first, next, then, etc. This means that the challenge of the organisational element is taken away from them until they have mastered the conceptual skill, which is likely to help reduce their barriers to learning.

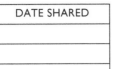

A suitable position in the classroom can make a huge difference to some learners' ability to take information in and to learn. This is particularly the case for those with attentional difficulties, sensory sensitivities and processing needs. Think about these learners when you are writing your seating plan and talk to them about where they will best be able to focus. Think about where in the room there are fewest noise and visual distractions, where they will best be able to see the board and which learners they are seated near to. Talk to them regularly about what is working and what isn't, and be prepared to make ongoing adjustments to the room and their position within it, to ensure they have best access to learning.

Learners with Dyslexia will not necessarily have lower cognitive ability than other learners – in many cases, it is purely their phonological processing that is the barrier. Therefore, be wary when you are differentiating that you are not giving easier work to learners with Dyslexia. Instead, think of ways to give the same level of challenge but in an accessible format. Simplify language, pre-teach vocabulary, help with reading, give alternative ways of recording answers – but aim to keep the level of conceptual and intellectual challenge in line with their underlying academic ability.

If speed of working is the issue, either give a reduced number of questions or tasks, or give more time and encourage them to use it!

DATE SHARED

Learners with Dyspraxia and co-ordination difficulties may struggle with aspects of practical lessons, including undressing and dressing for PE (particularly buttons, ties and shoe laces) or use of equipment in DT (using scissors). Have a chat with them about what they find difficult and what might help, and be on hand to support where needed.

When planning for newly-arrived learners with EAL, try to focus on two or three key words and concepts per lesson that you would like them to master. Make sure that you show picture clues for these every time you show or say the word, so that they can grasp the meaning. It is also worth ensuring that you have a way of translating these words into their first language, either by seating them with a peer who speaks the same language, or by having access to a bilingual dictionary or to an internet translator using a laptop, iPad or handheld device.

Often, learners with anxiety difficulties or who are on the Autism Spectrum appear to 'keep it together' during the school day and then display all their anxieties when they get home. This can mean that families bear the brunt of challenging behaviours or of emotional meltdowns and distress. Do not assume that a learner who appears okay, is okay, since often their level of anxiety leads to them feeling unable to show or manage their difficult feelings when with others. As a result, they can then display these when in the safe space of the home. If you have any sense that a student may be struggling with overload from the school day, liaise with the family, as well as asking them directly. There are often very simple steps that can be agreed together to reduce the general level of anxiety that school can cause.

DATE SHARED

Often learners with hearing impairments will need to be considered first when you are writing a seating plan; they may need to be seated near the teacher or with their stronger ear facing the class. Find out the specific needs of your hearing-impaired learners before you write your seating plan, so that you can get this right from the outset.

DATE SHARED

Assessments of all types can be highly-anxiety provoking for many learners with mental health difficulties. This can include formal exams and assessments, speaking and listening activities, as well as graded or levelled written work. You can help minimise learners' anxieties by acknowledging that lots of us find assessments scary and that is quite normal; discussing with them what the 'flashpoints' of their own anxiety are and making plans to manage these; returning written feedback in a timely manner and using clear and supportive, non-judgemental phrasing; and by reminding learners that exams and assessments are important but are not the only thing that will help them to achieve their goals in future life. Although learners' mental health needs can be complex, we should never underestimate the importance of a general atmosphere of support and encouragement for the learners we teach.

 © 2018 *Essential Tips for the Inclusive Secondary Classroom*, Whittaker, Hayes, Routledge

Practical, kinaesthetic and visual materials are stored away in many departmental offices but rarely used! Games, costumes, models, card sorts, artefacts and objects can all contribute powerfully to the learning experience, since they make information concrete and immediate rather than purely abstract, and are therefore more memorable for learners. If you can, take time as a department to dig out what you've got hidden away and make a real effort to use them to enhance your lessons this term.

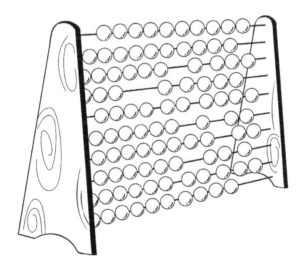

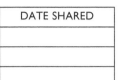

If you have any learners with physical disabilities in your classes, aim to keep a positive mindset about what they will be able to do, and never assume that they won't be able to take part in an activity without exploring this with them first. These conversations can take place from the outset: Are there roles that they are more comfortable with within the classroom, and are there peers who they prefer to work with? In time, you can then discuss with them what support they will need to widen who they work with and the roles that they can take on.

All learners with sensory needs and ASC are different; some may find the noise of the corridors unbearable, while others may not be bothered by it; some may find the smell of an old classroom highly distracting, while others may not notice this at all. It is really important therefore to get to know the individual and to find out what sensory demands are particularly challenging for them. You can then come up with a plan to help them manage these in your lessons, such as, for example, being allowed to work outside the room for extended writing or using headphones to block out noise while typing or to leave the lesson five minutes early to avoid the noise of lesson changeover.

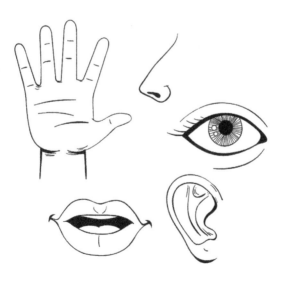

Some learners in your classes may have speech production issues, which make it difficult to understand them. This can feel uncomfortable for staff in terms of knowing how best to handle their difficulties, particularly when staff and peers may not always understand what the learner is saying. There are a few strategies that can help here. Firstly, always offer the learner a turn in class discussions; being encouraging but not insisting that they speak. Where it is not clear what they are trying to say, scaffold by giving them two options for them to choose from e.g. 'Was it _____ or _____?' Lastly, don't be afraid to tell them if you haven't understood and ask if they can tell you again, show you what they mean using movement or gesture or draw a quick diagram or picture to clarify.

© 2018 *Essential Tips for the Inclusive Secondary Classroom*, Whittaker, Hayes, Routledge

An over-reliance on text books in the classroom can prove a real barrier for many learners. Often the reading age of these books, even those targeted at learners in KS3, is above 15 years, meaning that they are not accessible to many learners in a class. Furthermore, the fact that learners can't use active reading strategies (such as highlighting key words, annotating with notes and pictures, etc) can also prove a real barrier for many. If you are using a text book in your lesson, it is worth thinking about ways of overcoming these barriers. You might choose to photocopy and enlarge a page for a group of two or three learners to actively read together, with specific information, ideas or words to look for and underline as they read. Or, you could scan / photograph and display the page on the whiteboard, so that you can read the body of text as a class and learners can come to the front and underline key points on the board.

DATE SHARED

Some learners with Visual Impairment will struggle to see even quite large greyscale pictures, as pale grey and white are not always contrasting enough to be seen clearly. Always check whether they can see the picture and tell you what it shows; if not, then describe to them and in future use your computer's 'edit' options to increase the level of contrast of such pictures.

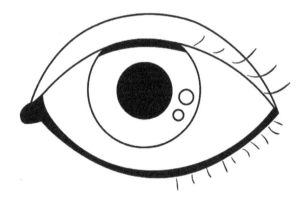

© 2018 *Essential Tips for the Inclusive Secondary Classroom*, Whittaker, Hayes, Routledge

Learners who find it hard to focus and concentrate will be more engaged in lessons if you can include kinaesthetic activities – tasks that allow them to work physically; to move and manipulate, to be practical and to make and create. For example, they could help you to model an activity to the class; they could create a practical product (maybe recorded by photograph or film) rather than a written response; they could show others what they have done once it is finished so that the 'product' is the demonstration itself. Such activities, if planned well, will allow them to show their grasp of the lesson content and is more likely to 'hook' them into the learning.

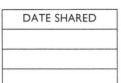

DATE SHARED

Learners with ASC will struggle with unexpected changes to routine – for example, supply teachers, unannounced assemblies, sudden tests and projects can all cause confusion and distress. As much as possible, try to prepare them for any changes to routine as this will minimise their anxiety. Ideally, remind them of the change more than once in advance and check whether they have any questions about what is going to happen. This will reduce the chance of them feeling stressed and anxious and the associated behavioural difficulties that can then result.

Make sure that displays in your subject area and classroom reflect the full range of difference and diversity in your school – ensure that you include representations of people of different ethnicities, people with a range of disabilities and impairments, people of different genders and sexualities and reference to varying cultures and languages. Actively plan for this and be prepared to challenge where it isn't happening!

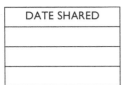

DATE SHARED

In Maths lessons, learners with Dyscalculia will need explicit teaching of checking strategies so that they can monitor the accuracy of their own work at each stage of a calculation. Model self-checking whenever teaching a new operation, and if necessary show them several ways to check whether their answer is right, so that they have a range of strategies available to them.

DATE SHARED

Many learners respond better to certain fonts, background colours and sizes of text over others, and this is particularly the case for those with Dyslexia and Visual Impairment. Talk to them about which of these are easier to read, and bear this in mind when preparing PowerPoints and worksheets. If a student shows a marked difference in performance with a particular combination of font, background colour and size of text, then liaise with the SENCO to let other staff know, so that these can also be adopted in other subjects.

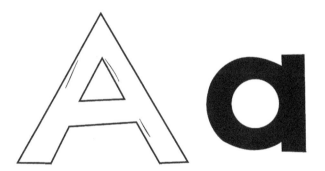

DATE SHARED

It can be very helpful to have all resources that learners will need in one easily accessible area of the room, ideally clearly labelled and kept in the same place week by week. Not only can this be generally helpful in creating a calm and organised classroom environment and reducing 'wandering', it can be particularly beneficial for those with Special Educational Needs. For example, learners with Dyspraxia, Physical Disabilities and Visual Impairment will greatly benefit from everything being in one area as this reduces the need for them to travel around a busy classroom and those Autism Spectrum Conditions will respond better to the predictability of a clear and consistent system.

DATE SHARED

When you have newly-arrived EAL learners, be aware that they may have cultural norms with regard to schooling, which are at odds with those you are used to. For example, some teachers may insist that learners look them in the eye when they are being spoken to, whereas, in many cultures, looking a teacher in the eye is considered to be inappropriate and rude. A quick search online can mean that you are more aware of the norms and expectations your learners bring with them, and therefore minimise the chance of misunderstandings.

Learners with trauma and difficult histories can only heal when they have the chance to build positive and respectful relationships with others. It is important that they have the opportunity to have time with their key adults in school on a regular basis. It is also vital that they don't have to 'play up' in the classroom to be sent out in order to get access to their key adult, as this simply reinforces negative patterns of behaviour. If you sense that this is happening with a learner you work with, get together with involved colleagues and come up with a structured and boundaried plan to allow the learner some time with their key adult each week, ideally to celebrate positives as well as to explore the week's challenges.

At some point, there are likely to be learners in your classrooms who have unidentified hearing problems. Be aware of the signs of a hearing problem so that you can ask pastoral staff to raise this with the family if necessary. Some of these are obvious, such as speaking more loudly than usual or appearing not to always hear well in the classroom. Others may be less obvious; for example, if a learner appears to always need to look very intently at the speaker in order to hear, seems to not be paying attention or taking information on board, has unclear speech or moves their head to one side (the stronger ear) when listening.

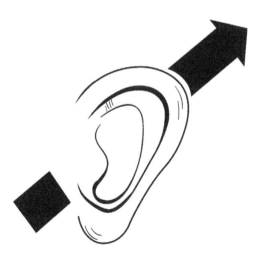

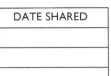

DATE SHARED

The fear of being publicly exposed or 'forced' to participate in front of peers can be highly-anxiety provoking for some learners – for example, 'team picking' in PE, or reading aloud in class, or being compelled to stand at the front of the room and present publicly, while seeming relatively insignificant to us as adults, are the kind of situations that can easily provoke an anxious learner into school refusal. Be aware of this and try to foster an environment of positive encouragement rather than one that is likely to provoke anxiety and fear.

DATE SHARED

Whenever giving an instruction to the class, always check that learners are clear about what they have to do, particularly those with SEND or EAL. Often learners will listen attentively and appear to have understood, but actually may not have the self-checking strategies to identify information they have missed. Always ask three or four learners (with hands down!) to repeat back to you what they need to do before getting the class started on any task. Use these learners' responses as a 'barometer' of the class's understanding, as well as an opportunity to repeat the key information to everyone once more.

For learners with sensory sensitivities and ASC, loud and unexpected noises such as fire alarms can be really traumatic and, at the least, can lead to feelings of being overwhelmed and at worst, to huge meltdowns. Have a plan in place as to how you will support any learners with those needs in your lessons if there should be a fire alarm. This could be as simple as having ear defenders or even earplugs or headphones on hand for children with sensory difficulties to reduce the noise of the alarm. Learners' with Autism Spectrum Conditions may benefit from advance preparation so they know what to expect; this can include social stories, structured role play and short films that show what to expect.

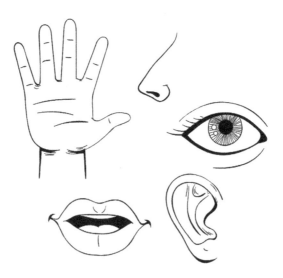

If you have teaching assistants in your classes, making sure that expectations and processes are agreed from the outset (for example, with regard to learners' behaviour) can really help to avoid problems in future. If there should be any issues, then make sure that your communication with each other is always as supportive and respectful as possible in front of the learners, and that any issues are dealt with outside of the classroom and away from the class.

Some learners with Learning Difficulties or who are on the Autism Spectrum can really struggle with theory of mind, the ability to imagine views other than their own. You can help them to develop this skill by allocating roles, which require them to think in a specific way for a group task. Edward de Bono's Six Thinking Hats can be a useful way in, with each learner taking on one way of thinking for a task from managing, information, emotions, discernment, optimism and creativity. Give them prompt questions for each way of thinking and praise when they manage to generate ideas within the strand they have been allocated.

Insisting that learners read aloud to the class when they do not want to, or can't, feels humiliating to those who have difficulties with reading – it will not help them improve and can often serve to alienate them further from the subject, from you as a teacher, and from the experience of school in general. The best approach is to encourage every student to take their turn in reading, but give everyone the right to 'pass' – those who are confident to read aloud will do so, those who are on the cusp will feel supported in time to have a go and those who have literacy difficulties will pass and listen to their peers read instead. This situation is likely to be far more conducive to engagement and learning than one where learners feel 'put on the spot' and exposed in front of their peers.

We often assume that writing tasks should be completed by learners on their own, meaning that many learners rarely see another person's writing or get access to their thought process as they write. Paired or small group writing can therefore be a very powerful way of developing learners' understanding of the topic at hand and of how this might be represented in writing. Giving out roles and rotating these at intervals means that nobody gets sidelined or is able to be overly dominant!

Learners with Visual and Hearing Impairments can sometimes be reluctant to wear their supportive aids, such as glasses and hearing aids, in school. Often, they are worried about appearing 'different' to their peers or about being teased or bullied. This then creates a barrier to their learning as they are not able to access lessons. You can help this by ensuring that any comments or teasing are dealt with rather than ignored, and, if you notice that a learner is not using their supportive aids, having a conversation with them away from the classroom about what the issue is to see whether there are any steps you can take that might help. If it becomes an ongoing issue, liaise with pastoral and Learning Support Teams to see whether a joined-up approach is necessary.

DATE SHARED

Learners who are currently residing with family members or are in the care of the Local Authority may not have the same access to the necessary resources to undertake work outside of school as those who are living with their birth family in terms of space and support, especially if there have been several and frequent moves. Plan for this within homework and individual learning projects by exploring with pastoral and support staff if there are homework / additional learning classes outside of scheduled lessons, or alternatively explore with the young person if it would be useful for them to complete work such as this in your classroom after school on a scheduled day. This can help to give them a sense of stability and reduce concerns they may have about where work can be completed. They could also be given a drawer or box to keep some items in, which gets locked away each night, again reinforcing a sense of security.

Many learners with ASC, EAL and Language Difficulties will not easily be able to make sense of metaphors and figures of speech. We frequently use phrases like 'eyes on the board' and 'a step in the right direction' in our classrooms without thinking about them, yet for learners who are using language in a more literal way, these can be bewildering and confusing. Be aware of this and, if you use an abstract figure of speech, make sure you also explain clearly and in simple and concrete terms what you mean by it.

DATE SHARED

Learners with SEND are frequently under-represented in extra-curricular clubs and activities. There may be many reasons for this, such as feeling that this level of specialist knowledge is 'not for them', to needing support to select and organise themselves to attend a club or activity. If you run any clubs, ask yourself whether these are attended by learners with SEND, and to think about what you could do to increase their participation – could you speak to the parents and learners to see whether they would like to attend? Could you arrange for them to be collected for the first week and brought along? Could you arrange for them to bring a friend as support? Think about what the barriers are and think creatively how you might be able to overcome them!

Learners with mathematical and general Learning Difficulties, even at secondary school age, can really benefit from being given diagrams and visual representations for mathematical operations. For example, addition can be presented as a number of objects being grouped with a number of other objects, or fractions can be presented as a pizza or cake being divided between a number of friends. This means that learners not only learn the operation and process, but also that they have a deeper understanding of the concepts they are using and their applications.

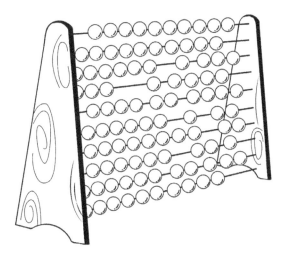

DATE SHARED

If you are teaching complex contextual information with lots of detail, many learners will benefit from the use of pictures as well as written information to help them to access and understand. Consider using storyboards to explain or summarise narratives, historical events, or scientific processes, and include thought bubbles / speech marks and captions to give the information some detail and depth.

Instead of giving your learners lists of instructions, consider using a flowchart or process diagram which shows the order each task needs to be completed in. If this is displayed on a PowerPoint slide, you can also print that slide onto paper so that some learners can also have it in front of them and tick of each stage. Learners with MLD, Dyspraxia, ADHD and ASC are particularly likely to benefit from an individual paper copy.

DATE SHARED

It is likely at some point that you will have newly arrived learners in your lesson who cannot read and write in English; some will also have no literacy skills in their first language. This calls for some creativity in your approach. When you are planning your lesson, choose five or six useful words from the topic for them to learn- these will probably be concrete nouns e.g. in a science lesson on recycling these might be metal, bin, plastic, glass, bottle, tin. You can then create a simple worksheet with a picture for each and labelled in a very light grey font which they can trace over. Or, you could give them pictures and words to cut up and match together, glue into their book and then practice writing and saying. If they can consistently master five new subject-specific words each and every lesson, then their English literacy and language will develop at a steady pace.

Be aware that when learners are stressed, their brains release high levels of the hormone cortisol. This means that negative experiences are recalled later on but without the necessary detail that will help the memory make sense. As such, stressful learning experiences are not only ineffective but, in addition, high levels of cortisol over an extended period of time can destroy neural pathways and can be detrimental to learning and cognitive performance. Therefore, perhaps counterintuitively, exams, tests, and presentations in front of the class can be damaging to the acquisition of knowledge rather than helpful, particularly for learners whose cortisol levels are already raised through earlier trauma. Be aware of this and make adjustments where you can; also, be sensitive to what support may be needed by individual learners to help them through these stressful experiences.

It can be very tempting to talk much more loudly to a person with a hearing impairment. However, be mindful that this can actually make things worse for your listener; it can be very uncomfortable for a hearing aid user if you shout as this sound is amplified for them. If in doubt, it is fine to ask them directly if you are talking too loudly or not loudly enough for them to hear you comfortably.

DATE SHARED

For many learners and families, the number one cause of school stress is homework. Many learners with anxiety are afraid of getting the work wrong and being punished for this, and many learners with Learning Difficulties worry about not knowing what to do, not remembering what is being expected of them, or not having time in the lesson to write the homework down before the bell goes. Teachers can take some simple steps to alleviate these anxieties. One simple step is to set the homework at the beginning of the lesson, rather than the end, so that there is time to write it down and time for questions. You can also provide a simple stick-in slip of paper with clear instructions, so that no information is lost in transcription. Finally, make sure homework is differentiated for any learning needs, so that learners do not have to struggle with work which is inaccessible for them.

Learners with Learning Difficulties may need help to develop their skills in making connections between what they learn in lessons, and life outside of school. Support them with developing these skills by making the relevance as explicit as possible; this can be as simple as asking open questions such as: Why are we learning this? What is the usefulness of this knowledge / these skills? How will this learning help you in your life? What is the purpose of this?

DATE SHARED

Many learners need time to adjust to the change in environment, subject and expectations when they change lesson. If you have learners who are repeatedly coming into your classroom 'out of sync' with the expectations of your classroom (very noisily following a practical subject, for example), then consider starting the lesson with 5 minutes of 'quiet time' where they do the same activity every lesson – silent reading perhaps, or a simple starter which is displayed on the board. This should help provide them with the space and time to adjust to the new environment, and give you the capacity to give individual reminders where necessary.

Learners with more significant Speech, Language and Communication needs may not always be able to find or say the words to tell you what they mean. This can be highly frustrating for them and can result in the listener feeling awkward and the learner giving up. If a learner is trying to express him or herself, don't put words into their mouth, be impatient with them, or try to suggest what they might want to say. Instead, give them thinking time or ask them to draw, show or to demonstrate what they mean.

Sometimes learners can struggle with understanding the different layers of meaning in a text – this is particularly true of those with EAL, language and communication difficulties, ASC and MLD. One easy way to dig deeper into what learners know is to use the framework of what, where, who, when, how and why to question their understanding. The first four of these will give you a sense of whether they are grasping the facts of the text (essential for understanding) and the last two will give you a sense of their level of inference (how well they are able to extrapolate meaning from the facts.) You can then work with them to fill the gaps of their understanding.

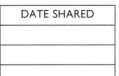

DATE SHARED

Learners who find it difficult to read words off the page (decoding), including those with Dyslexia, may benefit from text to speech technology. Text to speech technology can be accessed for free online, often as a 'plug in' which will read text aloud to learners as it highlights the words. A websearch for 'free text reader' will point you in the direction of the most recent packages available so that you or learners can download these to use in their lessons.

To encourage high quality writing in any subject, make sure you plan for learners to actively edit their work. Word processing serves this purpose well as you can add feedback in callouts or highlight sections for revisiting as they write. If they are handwriting, be explicit about your expectation that their first draft should not 'look neat' – you are expecting them to cross bits out, change bits, add bits . . . Showing them a screenshot of a heavily edited piece of writing will help them to be clear what you mean! You could also consider strategies such as 'editing flaps' (strips of lined paper stuck on at the margin) for extended improvements, or writing only on every other line to allow space for improvements.

If a learner with ASC or SEMH is struggling in your classroom, consider taking time to sit down with them (if possible with a supporting member of staff such as a TA) and explore a 'solution plan' – outline what the challenge is, what needs to happen, how it can happen, who can help, what it will look like, and how you will all know that it has worked. Write it down, in words, pictures or as a flow chart, and have a copy on the learner's desk when they come in so that they have a constant visual reminder. Praise them when they stick to the plan and try to 'check in' with the learner again at regular intervals to review how things are going.

Learners with attentional difficulties such as ADHD can really benefit from the use of 'fiddle toys.' This may seem counterintuitive since it may seem like an extra distraction, but in fact it can really help them to focus attention because it reduces the need to unconsciously 'search' for other things to focus on. Fiddle toys need to be used with agreements for use, such as holding it safely in their own hands and using it only when they need to. The fiddle toy should be agreed with the young person but it should be something which is quiet and not distracting to peers. This could include, for example, blu tack, a rubber spiky ball, pipe cleaners or even an elastic band around their wrist. Review its use regularly and monitor with the child whether it is having a positive impact.

Some learners who have ASC or ADHD can really benefit from having an individual workstation in or outside the classroom. This is a designated desk space which is only used by them, and which does not change in location or availability. It may have a screen at the back to reduce distraction and support concentration. You can even provide a greater level of structure with an 'in tray' and tickable task list of work to complete, and an 'out tray' for completed work. Learners who struggle working at a traditional classroom desk or table can really benefit from the predictability, structure and reduced sensory input that a workstation can provide.

DATE SHARED

When you are arranging any kind of school trip or visit, always do ensure that it is accessible for learners with physical disabilities and medical conditions, including those with behavioural needs such as ADHD. Schools are required to make reasonable adjustments for these young people to attend trips and visits, and there have been many cases nationally where parents have taken schools to tribunal under the Equality Act for excluding learners with additional needs from trips and visits. This includes schools who have not permitted these learners to attend, as well as some who have failed to make adjustments that would allow them to be included. You can plan for this by meeting with the SENCO at the earliest stage of planning, and making sure the necessary arrangements, adjustments, medical care planning and risk assessments are in place from the outset.

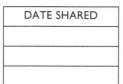

DATE SHARED

Explore the aspects of Maths that learners with Dyscalculia have most difficulty with, often they perceive their ability to be poor in all aspects of Maths, however, they can often have strengths in less numerical aspects of Maths, such as Shape, Space and Measure. By focusing on these areas of strength, you can shift a learners' negative perception of themselves as a mathematician and they may become more engaged in topics that they may have previously been resistant to.

Many learners with Dyslexia are less able to show the level of their knowledge and understanding in handwritten prose, meaning that written assessments are not always an accurate way of gauging their understanding of subject content. Think about whether there might be alternative ways for them to show what they know. For example, could they fill a grid or table with key points and ideas on the topic? Or could they be asked to write brief bullet points rather than prose?

For many learners, not least those with additional needs, routine is key. A clear and consistent routine for each lesson can reduce anxiety, help with behaviour, and ensure that key tasks and actions such as the register, setting of homework, and packing away, are not overlooked. You can even make the routine explicit by way of an agenda which is written on the board each lesson: e.g. Welcome and register with planners and pencil cases out; collect and set homework; starter; teacher input; task; feedback; plenary; packing away. Try this for a week and notice the effects!

Some newly-arrived learners will be happy to introduce themselves to the class- to talk about where they come from, their culture and so on. However, be mindful of the specific circumstances of learners who have had multiple school moves- travelling or military families, for example, or asylum seeker children. They may not yet be ready to process what has happened to them, or they may have been expected to do such introductions multiple times and may wish to just 'get on with it' with as little fuss as possible. If in doubt, as the student at the end of the first lesson what they'd prefer.

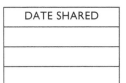
When writing, many learners with SEND and EAL needs find that 'getting started' is a real barrier. Help them through this by providing, or co-producing, five or six sentence starters that they can use to get them over the first hurdle. This will help to cue them in to tone and genre for the rest of the piece.

Learners can often really struggle with their difficult emotions, not always being able to identify, label or acknowledge feelings such as anger, shame, anxiety or frustration. You can help scaffold their emotional literacy in this area by using phrases such as 'I wonder . . .' to explore what may be going on for them and being curious and non-pressuring in talking about this with them. You can also describe to them the clues that brought you to that conclusion, with reference to their facial expression, tone of voice, chattiness and so on. Conversations such as this with a trusted adult will go a long way to developing a learner's ability to identify and come up with strategies for managing their challenging feelings.

Creative pursuits can be hugely beneficial for learners who are experiencing mental health difficulties such as depression or anxiety. For many young people, they can provide an invaluable opportunity to express complex thoughts and feelings in a less pressurised environment, and to take 'time out' from the pressures of the academic curriculum. You can help by encouraging your learners to pursue their own creative interests, such as music, art and craft, acting, or storytelling, and encouraging them to share what they have made as a source of enjoyment with its own value and merit.

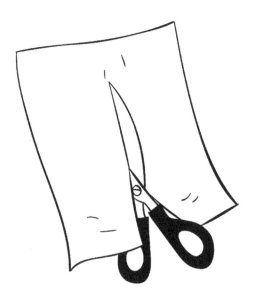

Activate learners' prior learning before starting a new topic by thoughtstorming together: What do we know about this subject? What don't we know yet? This can be recorded and dated in their books. They can then revisit the thoughtstorm during the course of the module to add their new learning in a different colour of pen. This is a simple process that will strengthen their metacognitive skills and contribute to a growth mindset since they will be able to see their learning as a process which is ongoing.

Music can have a visible impact on some learners' moods and ability to focus in the classroom. In particular, there is a correlation between the use of classical music in the classroom and learners' mood, concentration and attentiveness. Consider playing some classical music in your lessons this week, being aware that some might complain initially if they have negative associations with classical music! Observe how they respond once they have got used to it – if this is positive, then think about building this in more regularly.

Good organization can make such a difference in the classroom -it helps lessons to run smoothly and without interruption, increases predictability for learners, and communicates the message that, in this classroom, learning matters enough for us to take care of the space. Take ten minutes this week to refresh your classroom organization – label groups of resources and materials that learners may need in your lessons, and make sure that you have enough key items such as rulers, board markers, spare exercise books for new learners, spare pens, and so on.

DATE SHARED

A stern look and frown is often one of the most effective tools in a teacher or TA's toolbox and can be more powerful than words in some cases! Be aware however that learners with social communication difficulties including those on the Autism Spectrum may struggle to interpret facial expression alone. If this applies to learners in your classes, you will need to underpin your non-verbal communication with an explanation of how you are feeling, why you feel that way, and what you want them to do differently.

Help learners to access the key ideas of an informational text by teaching them to look for 'topic sentences' – the first sentence of each paragraph, which usually indicates the content of, or the argument contained in, the paragraph as a whole. Encourage your learners to read and mark these before tackling the entire text. This provides a good overview of the structure of the text and means that learners are better 'primed' to access the meaning than if they try to tackle the whole text in one go.

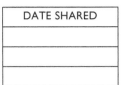

DATE SHARED

Computers can be used as valuable writing tools – writing doesn't always have to mean handwriting! Many learners, particularly those with Dyslexia or Dyspraxia, can transcribe their ideas much more effectively through word processing than handwriting, and so a range of recording tools can really pay off in terms of the quality of writing that is produced.

Many learners can benefit from the use of tactile materials in lessons, but those with Learning Difficulties, attentional difficulties, and Visual Impairments are particularly likely to benefit. Thing about how you can build some sensory aspects into your lessons this week: are there relevant subject materials which you could bring in for learners to touch and hold? Or is there some scope for model-making using a range of materials?

One of the most powerful tools we have as school staff is the positive phone call home. All too often in schools, parents and learners feel that we are quick to communicate what has gone wrong but slow to communicate the positive. This results in disengaged parents and learners and strained relationships all round. See if you can make at least one positive call home for every negative call – this could be to recognise an improvement, to acknowledge particularly good effort or to praise a specific piece of work or action. Learners love knowing that their energies are noticed and rewarded and are more likely to then invest in repeating those efforts and behaviours in future.

It can be tempting to avoid group work in the classroom because of the risk of social conflict and off-task behaviour. However, if structured carefully then most learners can really benefit from working in groups. Make it work by: investing time in planning the groups carefully beforehand; plan specific roles for the members of each group e.g. note-taker, chair, feedback leader, and so on; be clear from the outset what they are expected to show at the end of the task; give a pre-set amount of time for the task and keep it tight and pacy; and, lastly, be explicit about the teamworking skills that you are looking for, such as use of kind and respectful words and voices, everyone involved in the task, and reward groups where you see these.

When you communicate with a learner who has SEND, always try to speak to them directly rather than addressing questions or instructions to the adults who support them. Ignoring the learner in that way is considered to be exclusionary; it presumes that they have no capacity for direct communication in some form, and deprives them of the opportunity for direct communication with the school staff who are here to teach them. Sometimes you will need to make adjustments for communication, so liaise with your school's Learning Support Team to plan for these in advance.

For learners who arrive with negative associations with your subject, the use of games, quizzes and collaborative team activities can help to build up more positive associations over time. Think about how you can include such games and activities to consolidate learning – perhaps as part of a plenary or as a mid-lesson recap. Online tools can help you to create a plethora of games and activities including tailored wordsearches, random generators for team names, and even Who Wants to Be a Millionaire with subject-specific questions!

DATE SHARED

To support learners with literacy difficulties in the classroom, think about how you can use effective groupings to remove their barriers to learning. For example, in extended reading and writing tasks, you could create teams within the class and assign each student a role – one the reader, one the scribe, one the go-to helper, one the ideas generator, one the corrector, and adjust the amount of information given depending on their competency with the role. This means that learners have a structured way to collaborate on all aspects of reading and writing within their groups.

Many learners in secondary schools need support with fine motor skills, not just those with Dyspraxia. This can greatly affect not only handwriting, but dexterity with buttons, zips, laces and fastenings and accurate use of equipment such as compasses and rulers. Try to include a practical element in every lesson, however brief, and don't presume that poor performance is down to laziness or lack of effort, since accuracy with fine motor activities is very difficult for a lot of learners. Good activities to include are cutting, sorting, drawing and mark-making, kneading, and assembling; model ways to approach these and observe to see which learners will need extra practice in future lessons.

DATE SHARED

Think about how you can celebrate the contributions of different cultures within your subject area, making sure that diverse role models, cultures and languages are referred to in schemes of work, lesson materials and displays. This is just as important in schools with diverse student cohorts as in schools with less diversity.

For some learners with social and emotional needs, the feeling of not being 'heard' by adults can be a real trigger to spiralling behaviour. If they are struggling emotionally, take a moment to reflect back to them what they are communicating to you – e.g. 'I realise you are angry because I didn't choose you first. Let's make sure you go first next time.' Sometimes, this proof of being listened to with empathy and containment is enough to dampen down their feelings of frustration and reduce the spiral of escalation.

All staff can promote wellbeing by encouraging learners to 'take notice' of their own feelings, however uncomfortable they may be, and verbalising strategies for managing these. For example, before a test, you might say 'You are probably feeling quite nervous at the moment. That is very normal. I'm feeling nervous as well because I'm also going to be assessed on my teaching this week. One thing which really helps me feel less nervous is to really make sure I breathe deeply and slowly, so that I don't end up panicking and getting short of breath! Has anyone got any other ideas of ways to help with nervousness?' You can also help learners to recognise their own feelings by supporting them to label what they are going through; e.g. 'You seem to be feeling angry today – your face looks angry and you seem tense. Am I right?'

There are always going to be times when learners in our classes talk, whisper, fiddle, or are generally inattentive when we are speaking to the group. It can be very tempting at these times to keep talking regardless so that the lesson doesn't lose pace. However, it is really important to insist that learners' focus when you are talking to the class. Time you spend insisting on this at the start of the year will set an expectation that will help things run smoothly, and support learning, for the rest of the year. Model good listening and sitting up straight, looking at the speaker; using names to refocus individuals, and insist on silence when you are speaking. This will help create the kind of environment where all learners can listen and learn without distraction.

Young people are not always aware of the unwritten rules about social space, and this can be particularly true of those with learning difficulties or who are on the Autism Spectrum. Don't be afraid to be explicit about these rules. You can give individual or group recaps about personal space using the arm-length method in order to be as specific as possible. You can also teach learners a clear and respectful script for communicating with peers who get too close, so that they can address the issue without causing hurt or conflict.

Towards the end of term, as we and our learners become increasingly tired, it is easy to postpone our own rest and self-care until the holidays. The problem with this is that, as we become more exhausted, our bands of tolerance and patience reduce, and our general levels of stress and irritability increase. Our learners then match these moods in the classroom which can lead to difficult and challenging lessons. Take time in these final weeks of term to get rested before the holidays, so that you can look forward to a proper break with a positive frame of mind.

DATE SHARED

It is vital that you are ready and fully prepared for the needs and disabilities of next year's cohort before the day they arrive in your class. For example, if a young person with Dyslexia who needs coloured overlays joins your class, but you are not aware and so the overlays are not available for the first week, then this gives the student a substantial disadvantage to their peers during the vital first days of term. Use the last weeks of term to discuss next year's incoming learners with your SENCO and make sure you are ready for them – this will reduce workload in September and ensure a smoother start for your learners with SEND.

Use planned and targeted questioning to make sure that learners understand at all points of your lesson. If they don't, then pause your lesson plan and revisit the areas of misunderstanding. It can be very tempting to plough on regardless if you have planned a lesson, but it is vital to find time to address the gaps otherwise you are 'building on sand' in terms of developing their knowledge and understanding. If only a small number of learners are lacking in underlying knowledge and understanding, it may be that a small group 'catch up' session, either within or outside the lesson, or some creative timetabling with colleagues, means that you are able to work more intensively with that group in order to address the gaps and help them to be able to access the content of the lesson more effectively.

DATE SHARED

Often we assume that learners know what behaviours we expect, but for some learners, our core expectations of 'please' and 'thank you', the use of clean and respectful language, and respect for others' personal space cannot be assumed, because these may not be the norms they are used to. Try to be really explicit about what basic positive behaviours you expect – notice and label them when you see them in your lessons, and consider having a 'behaviour focus' for a week every so often; you could give team points for the sides of the classroom who show these most consistently and recognise them with a simple reward – this could even be as simple as getting to leave the classroom before the rest of the class that day!

One useful model of supporting reading is DARTS – Directed Activities Relating to Text. DARTS are strategies for getting learners to be active with reading and engaging with texts, and are useful in the classrooms of most subjects. Examples of DARTS might include giving learners a text with key words missing, which they then have to discuss and select in a pair or group; this forces engagement with a text and reduces passivity. Another example would be asking learners to write a suitable label for each paragraph of a text, and then discussing and giving team points for the most suitable labels. If you feel that DARTS might help your learners to engage with reading more effectively, a quick websearch will yield a large number of other strategies for you to try in your classroom!

DATE SHARED

Make laminated lists of key words with picture clues to help your learners as they write. You can make these by topic on a departmental basis so that they can be re-used; they are helpful for learners with a wide range of needs including EAL, Dyslexia, MLD and Speech, Language and Communication Needs and are an easy way to support all learners to learn and to use subject-specific language in your classroom.

When working with learners with SEMH or ADHD, it can be tempting to notice and try to correct every infringement they make, and to escalate through the behavioural policy at each stage. However, this approach is not likely to result in the behaviour you want: it is likely only to inflame the situation, sour the relationship and disrupt the lesson. Instead, think about which battles are worth picking now, and which can be quietly ignored and picked up on later in a low-key way and without an audience. For example, if a child is chewing gum, then stopping teaching, raising your voice and insisting they walk to the bin with an audience is far more disruptive than having a quiet work 1:1 when the class is settled and working. Know when to pick your battles!

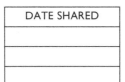
Students with ASC are likely to struggle with tasks which require free imagination, such as story writing and creating plays. Plan for this by starting the task with shared generation of ideas – perhaps the whole-class can contribute to a spider diagram of ideas on the board, or a thought storm with post-it notes on a large sheet. Alternatively, you could give the class an alternative option of creating a non-fiction story or recount.

Mental health problems can too often be treated as the 'poor relation' of other disabilities, and people with mental health conditions are often subjected to misunderstanding, stigma and other people's embarrassment. Make sure your classroom is a place where mental health is respected- avoid using terms such as 'mad', 'mental', 'OCD', and 'insane' flippantly. Instead, be prepared to invest some time in upskilling yourself so that you can talk clearly and confidently about mental health problems as and when the subject arises. The Young Minds, Mental Health Foundation and NHS websites are a good starting point for this.

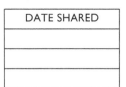

DATE SHARED

Learners with ASC can benefit if you can make everything visual for them. Make and use little visual picture cards when you want their attention, need them to listen or to prepare them for a transition such as change of task or the end of the lesson. Information presented visually is clearer, less ambiguous, can be revisited later and will also stay in their short-term memory for longer than information which is only given verbally.

When you are reading to the class from a PowerPoint and want learners to follow the text, you will need to provide support in order for all learners to be able to do this. You can do this by using a large meter ruler to point to or underline the line you're reading, or you can use a board marker to underline key words and phrases as you read so that they can keep track if they lose their place.

Aim to spend some time before any reading activity cuing learners in to the text's context. This could include reading and discussing the title and thoughtstorming associations and possible meanings; analysing pictures and subheadings, and making predictions in pairs as to what the text will contain. All of these strategies will ensure that your learners are cognitively primed and more ready to learn once they start reading, than if they approach a text with no prediction or engagement activities having taken place beforehand.

To build the trust and respect of our classes, it can be very powerful to acknowledge when you have made a mistake. This may sound counter-intuitive since it may sound as though this will threaten our authority and status within the classroom, but conversely it can serve the opposite purpose. Acknowledging our errors and mistakes on occasion can provide learners with an adult model of the values we want them to show – a willingness to correct mistakes, a flexible growth mindset, humility, honesty and respect. It also shows them confidence when mistakes are made, and so there is reduced satisfaction for them when they try to embarrass or humiliate teachers who make a mistake.

For learners with social anxiety, the thought of other learners getting to 'pick teams' and not being picked can be highly traumatic. Similarly, being asked to find their own groups to work in can feel very anxiety-provoking – what if nobody wants to work with them? Avoid this by planning groups and teams in advance – make them random and ideally mixed-ability, and change them each lesson to keep them fresh. This reduces the fear of being left out and increases an atmosphere of acceptance and inclusion in the classroom.

Our learners learn a lot about social and emotional literacy from the way they see us, as adults, react to certain topics and situations. When they observe us responding to a difficult or sensitive topic with silence or avoidance, this can be very confusing for learners as they don't always know how to interpret this. Therefore, we need to try to acknowledge and discuss tricky topics such as stress, religion and relationships in our lessons; allow learners to share questions and responses even if this makes us feel uncomfortable. If you need time to come back to them with an appropriate response, tell them that you really want to come back to that topic, and make sure that you keep your word so that learners know they can rely on you for the guidance they are asking for.

In departments where learners are taught in ability sets or where there are designated SEN classes, it can feel very difficult for those placed in bottom sets or SEN groups if attention is repeatedly drawn to this in front of them and their peers. As much as possible, deal with this sensitively and try not to discuss settings and groupings in front of learners. If learners have questions, it may be more appropriate to deal with these in a low-key way on a one-to-one basis rather than with a whole class.

Try to vary the way in which you read text in the classroom – for example, if you always read to the class, your learners are likely to very quickly 'switch off!' Think about whether learners could read in pairs or groups of three; or whether you could read around the class with learners happy to read tackling a sentence or two (specify in advance!) before passing on; or whether you ask volunteers to read a paragraph each – write their names on the board in advance so that they know which paragraph is theirs. Ensure that everyone is listening by telling the class you will be asking questions by name after the text has been read, and that they will need to be ready for these.

For learners with literacy or Learning Difficulties who are struggling with a specific spelling, being advised to 'look it up in a dictionary' can feel very hindering and demotivating – it slows them right down and they get even further behind their peers. You might decide to help them keep pace by just giving them the correct spelling and, where appropriate, praising them for their word choice.

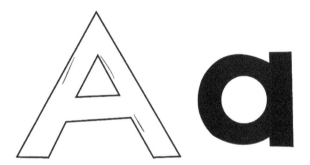

Working with young people who have complex emotional, social, learning and safeguarding needs can at times be as draining and stressful as it is, at other times, rewarding. Keep an eye on your own wellbeing and be aware of the risk of taking on too much emotional burden, as this is exhausting and unsustainable in the long term. Make sure you take advantage of the support of those you can talk to, whether colleagues within school, or friends and family outside of school. If you feel that the emotional strain is becoming unmanageable, there are many avenues of potential support including your GP, HR and employee support services, and specialist organisations such as the Teacher Support Network.

Many learners find it difficult to cope with less structured times such as break and lunch times. This can particularly be true for newly-arrived EAL learners, those with ASC, and those with social and emotional needs. There are many reasons for these difficulties; for some, the range of choices in less structured times can feel overwhelming; others feel bored easily and respond with poor behaviours and social conflict; some worry about who they will spend time with; many worry about being bullied, and some struggle with the less boundaried nature of these times of the day. If a learner in your care is struggling with this, you can support them by co-constructing a plan of what they are going to do, who they will spend their time with, and what the expectations are for behaviour. Note it down and revisit and review it with the learner at regular intervals.

Many learners with SEND and EAL are likely to be confused by the range of mathematical terminology that is often used interchangeably in lessons. It is vital that teachers of Maths are explicit in teaching the language of mathematics and use it clearly and consistently within lessons. A simple display of synonyms for functions e.g. addition, subtraction, multiplication and division can be really useful if it is referred to during teaching or whenever a new term is used.

If you have access to tablet computers in your department, then there is a huge amount that you can do with these to support the learning of learners with SEND and EAL. Online translators, filming of verbal summaries, speech to text software, text to speech software, online talking books and learning apps are constantly being developed and updated and have huge potential to overcome the learning barriers that learners may have. A websearch will guide you towards the most recent apps and programmes for the specific needs of your learners.

Many learners on the Autism Spectrum have specific areas of knowledge and interest. If you can spend time some time finding out what these might be for the learners you work with, and finding out a few facts about those topics, then you can use these to strengthen your relationship with those learners and also to engage them in tasks which may otherwise be less interesting to them.

It can be very difficult to get feedback and capture the thinking of learners who struggle verbally, either because they are socially anxious or withdrawn, or because they have speech, language and communication difficulties. One way in which you could overcome this is to use an 'exit ticket' system – at the end of each lesson, give learners a slip of paper and some time to note down their responses to given sentence starters. These could include: The most important thing I learnt today was . . . One thing I would like to know next is . . . I am not clear about . . . You can then collect these as learners leave the room and use them to inform your planning of the next session.

In secondary schools, we often default to handwriting as a way of showing knowledge but there are often alternative ways for learners to show their knowledge which allow those with literacy difficulties to show their learning and understanding more easily. Consider whether some learning could be recorded in an alternative way: by making minibooks, short films, podcasts, collages, thoughtstorms, photographs, labelled diagrams or models.

If you have a class which you find challenging, stressful, undermining, or unusually inconsistent in their mood and approach, it can be worth taking some time to reflect on the reasons for this and how you can make things feel more positive whilst you are with them, as a positive end to the school year can sometimes take some planning! One approach to try might be to 'take your emotional temperature' before and after you teach them for the next few lessons; are you feeling stressed before they enter your room, and how might you unintentionally be communicating this to them? Aim to make one or two specific positive changes each lesson, such as eye contact with the most difficult learner, or a compliment to another who is disengaged, or give a positive 'hook' to the whole class about how well they did on a previous occasion. Notice and reflect on whether these changes result in small-stepped improvements.

Be realistic about how long learners with ADHD will be able to focus. This is likely to vary hugely from task to task, but if you have observed that they are not able to concentrate on writing for more than 5 minutes, then expecting them to concentrate for longer periods than that is setting them up to fail. Instead, plan the lesson so that you 'chunk' focused writing into 5 or 10 minute sections interspersed with other activities which also contribute to their learning and understanding of the topic in hand. The benefit for you, your class and the student in question is likely to be more 'on task' time and fewer disruptions to learning.

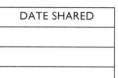

DATE SHARED

One way to effectively teach writing is to collaborate as a class to produce a 'model' piece of writing; for example, a report on an experiment etc. Pairs can contribute ideas by holding up a mini-whiteboard and you can gather the best and type these up and display them on the board, talking aloud your thought processes as you go. Print the finished piece and glue into books as a 'model' for future pieces. Make a note at the bottom which says, 'This model text was co-produced as a class on (date)' so that it is clear to parents and visitors what the text represents!

© 2018 *Essential Tips for the Inclusive Secondary Classroom*, Whittaker, Hayes, Routledge

Learners with Visual Impairments may be near or far sighted, and this will impact on the best seating position in the classroom in order for them to see the board. If you are teaching any learners with Visual Impairments next year, take time this week to check the details of their impairment and where they should best be seated in the classroom. This information will be held by the SENCO in your school.

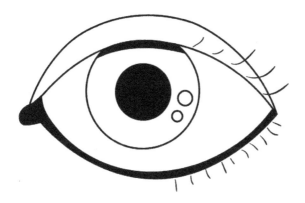

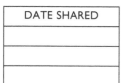

DATE SHARED

Young people with mental health difficulties need the chance to 'connect' with trusted adults and peers. Where possible, be available to listen, without trying to find an immediate answer or making a judgement of their situation.

Learners who find Maths difficult, including those with specific number difficulties such as Dyscalculia, can become easily distracted by superfluous resources around the room and on the desk in Maths lessons. Support them to focus by highlighting the necessary resources for the current lesson (by pointing or by placing and removing irrelevant ones) and if necessary change what is available to them as the lesson progresses and they need to use different materials. Scaffold their access to the visual supports to reduce their need to process this information, as this provides an additional cognitive load on top of the learning task itself.

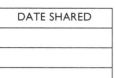

DATE SHARED

Never underestimate the value of using gesture and mime in helping learners with EAL to understand what you are talking about. As much as possible, try to exaggerate your hand movements and encourage them to look at you as you talk, by using their name. Although this can feel unnatural at first, it can be hugely powerful in both engaging learners and in communicating meaning.